Have Your Angels

Call My Angels

Have Your Angels

Call My Angels

Artie Hoffman

For a private psychic/medium reading in person, over the phone, Facetime, or Skype or to book a party, even or public speaking.
Contact information below.
732-778-7173
Artiehoffman.com
Artiehoffman@gmail.com
Facebook Artie Hoffman's Angels and Answers

ISBN: 9798593034120

FOREWORD

I honestly had no intention on writing a second book. The only reason why I did, is because when people who have read my first book, "Angels and Answers," have complained. Their biggest complaint was that there wasn't enough to read, they wanted more, they wanted to learn more about life's meaning and answers. I was so happy and humbled by the public's comments that between that experience and the driving force of my friend Valentina, it drove me to create more chapters for everyone to enjoy.

I have literally read for over 30,000 people in my life. While I am doing readings and when I am by myself, I get in that clear emotional /spiritual space where my spirit guides and angels communicate to me in my thoughts, bringing me all kinds of inspirational answers to share with the world. Even though the words and messages are coming from my mouth, it's like I am hearing them for the first time myself. When I am in that clear emotional/spiritual zone, messages come to me naturally, not that I have to drop acid or do mushrooms to get to that kind of high. Lol. However, when I am on that Spiritual High, it allows me to see clear visions while I read for people as well as while writing this book.

Nothing makes me happier than when someone comes up to me and says, "Thank you for making such a difference in my life. Your words and your positive energy have changed my life for the better, forever."

And, so, I turned, and I look up and I say, 'Calling All Angels!! Calling All Angels!! I need your help!! Please talk to me some more so I can tell the public what they need to know, and what they need to hear!! I can't do it without you Thank you!! Thank you!!'

So, you want to know and learn more about life?
Have your Angels call my Angels

ACKNOWLEDGEMENTS

I'd like to thank God and my Guardian Angels for giving me the strength and inspiration to be able to carry on with my life's purpose: helping, guiding, and counseling others, to bring them to a happier emotional state of mind with true life answers and meaning.

Even though we might not always think so, but God's timing is pretty darn good when it comes to bringing the right people into our life, at the right time. Again, I need to thank God for bringing my Heaven sent loving, unconditional friend, Valentina, into my life. It was her love and support that got me to write this book. Her words were. "Artie, your followers and your fans love you! They loved your first book; you have to write a second book! Come on, I will help you with whatever you need, whatever it takes, I will help you organize and edit your next book. All you have to do is write." And so, I did, and so she did, and our second book is now born, and we named her, "Have Your Angels Call Our Angels." Not only did Valentina's Love and words inspire me, so did my many friends' and clients' support as well with their loving thoughts and positive energy. Hope you enjoy reading this book as much as I enjoyed writing it.

May God Bless You!

GOD! THANK YOU FOR ALL MY BLESSINGS!

I feel so grateful to God for putting me in a position to be blessed as a messenger and healer, for giving me the ability and opportunity to serve the public and His children who seek out to reach me.

For all the years that I have counseled people, it's not just me or my personal thoughts that give people the emotional comfort and answers that they are looking for, It's God and the Angels that feed me all the answers and resources that I need to help others. I consider myself a messenger and a healer on behalf of God, and when God and the Angels share their thoughts and loving energy with me, I share all that with others.

When I put my hands on someone it's the love and power of God they feel through me, it's not just my touch they're feeling that makes people feel good, but the love of God as well. Most people can feel the calming, loving energy right away when I touch them. What is really cool is that there are times when I deliver messages to people, even though the words are coming out of my own mouth, I am hearing it for the first time myself. I am so amazed by some of the beautiful messages that are so meaningful and powerful... I'm like, Holy crap! I have to write all these awesome messages down now or I will forget what I just said!

Bless your past for all the lessons you learned and that you no longer need to endure the hardships of your yesterdays.

Stop recreating in your thoughts what once was and make your today's as pleasant as possible by listening to the kind of music you enjoy listening to or going to nice places you enjoy visiting.

You can no longer control circumstances of your past, but you do have control of how you choose to live your today and tomorrow.

You may have some weaknesses going on within your body or within your life, but are you going to allow those weaknesses to override the positivity of your strengths so that you can still make things happen or make things better.

It is your choice. God gave you the Blessing of "free will."

The reason why God makes things a little more difficult for you at times is because when things were extremely uncomfortable yet still somewhat doable, you did not have the faith and strength to move forward into a better situation for yourself. You fell into complacency.

Being that you kept on procrastinating, God took over and created situations to become even more difficult, to make you more uncomfortable, to motivate you, to get you out from where you no longer belong.

Now you get it!?!

Misery doesn't appreciate or recognize the beauty in anyone, especially within itself.

Miserable people feel if you were actually to see the true value and beauty that lies within you, you would no longer want to stay living in their lower vibration, in their world of misery.

Rather than support you and love you, they put you down to make themselves feel bigger or better, but in reality, they're only making themselves look and feel uglier.

Misery loves company and doesn't want you to leave.

You can't save someone who can't or doesn't want to save themselves, but you can save yourself. You paid your dues; you don't have to stay living in an emotional or physical hell anymore.

Your Angels are waiting for you to step into the world of beauty and happiness where you belong.

HEY BUTTERFLY

Be kind to yourself, don't allow yourself to stay stuck in your cocoon.

Don't be seduced again and again by the empty promises and lies for what the dark side of life only has to offer you.

You may have gotten used to it over the years, I understand, but it's time for you to grow and move on, to be where you belong.

If you're wise and smart, you'll be kind to yourself and choose the path of light over darkness.

The transformation of switching over might be a painful process while the dark side is fighting to keep your soul.

Remember misery loves company.

However, that pain of inconveniences is just temporary during the time of transformation, turning Darkness into Light.

Like the Butterfly that transforms, you'll have the beauty of love, light, freedom and happiness that will shine over on you forever while you spread the beauty of your wings.

Listen to your gut and soul.

Invest in your long term of freedom and happiness.

Don't allow yourself to be seduced by your ego side, buying into the illusion of short term

happiness of what the dark side only has to offer you.

Trust - Believe - Faith

Happiness awaits you ♥□♥□♥□♥□♥□

Why 5 hearts? Because the number 5 represents changes and changes represent transformation.

SACRIFICE AND JOY

Is it really a Sacrifice when you give up someone or something that brings you pain when you are going after what it is you love or desire in the big picture of life?

This is My Journey to Grow:

I became wiser and stronger through the journey of my pain.

My heart and soul can see what's real and what's not real. I can see and understand the reality of life and the meaning of what true Love really is.

I don't have to remain stuck in someone else's limited way of thinking and believing. Their reality no longer has to be mine.

For me to allow others in my personal space and place, they must Earn the Love and Respect I now have for myself.

I will no longer give my personal power away to others who don't deserve it.

You must be one special person if I allowed you in my personal life,

that means I really Love and Trust you.

How do I Know When I Truly Love Someone?

When it makes me happy to make them happy or when it makes them happy to make me happy.

My Heart Sings when I see someone else smile because of something I did for them. I feel happy I feel safe in their company and in my own.

I come to understand I no longer have to keep on re-experiencing the pain of others and sacrifice my happiness.

I did my part and now I have to honor myself so that I can be the best I can be, not just for myself but, also for the sake of other people who are important to me in my life.

Through my journey of pain, my growth, my awakening, I found out that God, My Angels and loved ones in Heaven never gave up on me.

By the constant reminders of signs, they leave me, I realize, I am never alone.

Thank you, God, for your Blessings!

The ultimate happiness isn't just about attaining and accomplishing the success of your goals, true fulfillment of happiness is when you have that special someone to share your successful moments with.

Loyalty, support, and dedication can keep love going on forever in a relationship. Taking anyone or anything for granted can end all of that in a heartbeat. The love and respect that you give is the love and respect that you deserve.

All fears and anxiety go away from your life when you let go of your expectations.

Just because you can tolerate pain doesn't mean you have to take it.

Creating solutions for the public and doing something about it will improve the quality of your life. Where there are problems in life, there are opportunities.

It's always nice to be rewarded in the material world. It is even nicer and more rewarding when you make a positive difference in other people's lives.

TO BE HAPPY AND IN CONTROL

Even though you know you're a really nice person, the reason you might still feel bad about yourself on the inside, is because you feel that no matter what you do for other people, it'll never be enough according to their expectations. You feel that people may get mad at you, not so much because of what you do to them, but what you don't do for them. You want to know who really loves you for you unconditionally and who are the ones who love you with conditions or who really loves you at all? Stop performing and doing things for others for a short period of time and you will see people's true colors. You will see who still stands by you and respects you and you will see those who get mad at you or ignore you since you stopped doing things for them. Remember, these people are the ones that rarely do for you.

Do you love me for me or just what I do for you?

If you want to feel self-respect, you need to say "NO" when something doesn't feel right for you. If you simply can't or don't want to do something, simply say, "I can't, I don't want to, No!" By doing this, by being this way, you give yourself back your own power.

Why should you keep performing for others if they are not reciprocating to you in the same nice way or showing you sincere appreciation?

If people keep pushing you when you say "No!" to them, they do not care about you or your feelings. They only want what they want and care about themselves, not you. If you keep performing according to other people's expectations and demands while they treat you like garbage, why should they stop? Their lives aren't changing, it isn't their fault, it is yours! You are the one continuously accepting this bad behavior and performing to please them.

When you take a stance and change, you force other people to have no other choice but to change as well. If you are chasing other people's approval, then you aren't approving of yourself.

You want others to respect you?
Start respecting yourself.
Love thyself. Respect thyself.
Honor thyself.

Whew!

PERSONAL HISTORY AND TRADITION

Knowing about your past gives you more meaning and understanding of who you really are. You'll find it interesting to know about your family and ancestors' background, who they were and where they came from. You will have a deeper understanding about yourself and family, why you're in certain situations in your life based on your background and family history.

Also, keeping traditions whether it be family-based or spiritual/religious-based. This is a way to keep the memory alive to show appreciation to the people who were directly or indirectly responsible for your lifestyle or your way of thinking on some level. The people of your past gave you their legacy which helped mold you in the way that you are today and in the way that you think. For medical reasons, it's good to know about your past.

Do you want to know why you are so talented?

Why you're so smart?

Why you are so crazy?

Take a good look at your past history and you will find a lot of answers as to why you are the way you are.

WHEN DID I MAKE YOU SMILE, GOD?

-Was it when I got my new car?

-No, I smiled when I saw how many people you gave a ride to when they really needed it.

-God, were You proud of me when I bought my new home?

-I was happy for you when you bought your new home. I was proud of you when you let people into your home and how good you made them feel when they walked in.

THE ART OF HEALING

The fastest way of healing is coming to a place of acceptance and coming from a place of forgiveness. Accept people for who they are and not what you want them to be or how they should be. You can adjust yourself and how you choose to deal with others, you can even choose not to deal with them at all. You can give someone warm and friendly advice on how they can step up their game, but if they choose not to be a certain way, you need to accept that. An exception to this rule would be the way you're raising your kids, teaching them the difference between right and wrong. However, as far as partners, friends, family members, and co-workers are concerned, those rules do apply.

Forgiveness.

If you find it difficult or impossible to verbally express to others how they have hurt you, if you want to express your true feelings to them and express your thoughts or pain, you should hand write a letter. Whether you give them the letter or not, after you physically write it, read it out loud when you are by yourself as if they are standing right in front of you. At the end of that letter, let them know that you forgive them.

I don't give you any more power over me, to emotionally control me with anger. I release my anger and resentment toward you so I can be the best person I can be. Not only do I forgive you, I also forgive myself for allowing our situation/relationship to continue the way that it did for as long as it did. I forgive the both of us and wish you well, goodbye!'

After you have done all of this, take your handwritten letter and burn it outside allowing the smoke signals to go to Heaven. You should then feel a beautiful sense of release. You are no longer in emotional shackles; you are emotionally free from that person and that burden.

AMEN!

MEANING OF LOVE

Love has no Religion,

Love has no Boundaries,

Love can only heal you

when you open your heart to receive it.

SPEAKING THE TRUTH, BEWARE!!!

Most people are not strong enough to hear the truth. They want to hear how they want the truth to be, not necessarily the reality of it. Sometimes being brutally honest is the best way to be with some people; but then again, being compassionate in a loving way, when telling the truth is also another way to get the point across. A lot of it depends on the personality of who you are dealing with, or the circumstances you're dealing with. Try to use your best judgment when you have to lower the boom when you're telling someone your truth.

They say honesty is the best policy, but other people might think you suck when speaking your truth. That's only because you're not measuring up to their expectations when you're trying to explain to them how you really feel.

Timing is very important of when to say what and to whom. It might be a great idea to get someone else's support and opinion on how to deliver your news if you feel overwhelmed and stressed when delivering your truth.

If someone is respectful and brave enough to tell you the truth, especially when you asked for it, it would be very wrong of you to emotionally beat them up and yell at them when they are telling you the truth. What is their incentive being honest and truthful to you, if you're going to freak out on them? It's normal for you to get upset when hearing the truth but you shouldn't be attacking the other person when the truth is being told. At least now you know the truth of the matter of what you are dealing with. Would you rather them lie to you? So at least give them credit and appreciation for being honest with you, or should they just tell you what you want to hear even though it's not the truth.

Telling the truth is a lot like going to the dentist it can be very painful when you're going through it but the end result is to have a healthy situation on your hand when it's all said and done and it might take time until the throbbing goes down. LOL.

AMAZING GRACE

No kind act is ever hidden from the eyes of God. You might not get the love, credit, or appreciation you deserve from the people you are sharing your love and kindness with, but God surely notices.

What happens when this occurs is that God rewards and Blesses you with the love, kindness, and generosity from other people or situations that do come into your life.

What do I mean by this?

Example:

Let's say you gave your time, money, and positive energy to the people of the East Coast and in return you got next to nothing from them; no appreciation, no payback, no nothing...but, how God and The Universe rewards you, is by giving you Blessings and love from the people of the West Coast.

Getting angry and upset with the people you've just helped is a natural reaction when you're not being appreciated, but in reality, you're not paying attention to all the other great things that are happening in your life because you're so upset with the people who you feel owe you natural reciprocation on some level.

You're wasting your positive energy into a negative vibration. The more attention and energy you put into the negative, the longer you keep the negativity alive. So, let it go!! You can remain upset and angry for a long time and by your own choice. By having a bad attitude, you'll end up ruining the rest of your day, week, month, year, or life!!!

It is not necessary to get on everyone else's emotional negative bullshit drama stage. There are so many people who say, "I'm just trying to be nice to everyone and I keep getting crapped on by everyone from all directions." The reason why this happens to nice people is because you allow yourself to get caught up in other people's karma by getting too involved. You don't know when enough is enough. If you aren't respecting your own boundaries, neither will anyone else.

When you try to save others too many times, you're not allowing them to learn from their own choices and mistakes. To spot help them out of a jam is cool and wonderful, but when you're helping out too much where it is affecting your happiness and/or lifestyle, then that's not the best move for you.

To help someone who has enthusiasm of some kind of a plan, or they have a desire to better their life circumstances, that's a winning positive move on your part to want to help that someone out. If you're putting good money or positive energy into someone who doesn't want to help themselves, you're wasting your time and energy and it will end up costing you your happiness.

It is great to help others, just understand when enough is enough. While you're being generous to others, respect and honor yourself along the way. If the people you are loving and/or helping out are not showing you sincere appreciation and just wanting more and more, you need to respect yourself and stop giving!

If you're chasing after other people's approval, then you're not approving of yourself... and it is by your own choice, by giving too much of yourself without positive energy being returned will take away your self-esteem and self-confidence.

Do yourself a favor, take care of yourself while you're taking care of others and just know when enough is enough.

WHAT KILLS AND WHAT HEALS

It is our expectations that we place upon other people or situations that is the number one killer of our heart and soul. If you don't place high expectations upon other people, you can never get hurt or disappointed.

People may promise you the world, whether it be personal or about business, and in the moment, they can very well mean every word that they just said to you, but all of a sudden circumstance arise in the short or long coming that they could not foresee that are keeping them from their original promise to you. Maybe they over promised you what they can't deliver and the reason why they can't or didn't is because time just didn't allow them to fulfill their original promise to you. Maybe they just didn't want to disappoint you in that given moment, so they told you exactly what you wanted to hear to avoid an argument or sad ill feelings. Maybe you are placing too many high expectations onto someone else's character or ability where they are either not willing to pull through or they are incapable of pulling through.

So, wouldn't you say, it now becomes your fault instead of theirs? You're putting too much value and credit into someone who isn't going to deliver. When are you going to realize you can't squeeze blood out of a stone? Stop allowing yourself to get so upset and disappointed about a person or situation who has wronged you in the past. If you got screwed over before, what makes you think it won't happen again with that same person or situation? You want to keep on making up excuses on their behalf of why things went wrong at your emotional or financial expense? Don't try to keep on jump starting a dead battery. That's who they are by nature, it is not about you. It's time for you to respect yourself and move on.

HOPE FOR THE BEST AND PLAN FOR THE WORST

When people get married and say their vows to one another, both parties (husband and wife) for the most part, have every intention of keeping their vows sacred, when they say, "until death do us part."

According to religion, those words mean until one of you physically dies.

According to the Spiritual world those words mean, if one of your hearts emotionally dies in the relationship, "until death do you part."

As people grow in life, while being married, they often times develop new relationships through work or personal activities, such as going to the gym, playing sports, mutual friends, or classes in school, etc. Any young couple that starts a relationship together can only hope that their love and respect for one another is strong enough to endure all the changes and challenges that life has in store for them and their deep love for one another remains the same.

The bottom line is, God wants all of us to be happy. It is by our personal choices of what we are willing to accept or not accept. Unfortunately, too many of us choose to accept bullshit circumstances to remain in our lives. Rather than standing up for ourselves, too many times we allow others to walk all over us or take advantage of us.

If we don't nip problems or issues in the bud by having a healthy conversation with the ones who are being disrespectful, our problems will continue to become more and/or larger. If we don't have that talk then the resentments kick in, and we start to disrespect one another in countless ways. Love and respect starts to slowly dissolve.

While the other people in our lives, who aren't connected to our problems, start becoming much more appealing because we are sharing the best of who we are while others are sharing the best of themselves with us. People like to be in the company of others where there is some kind of fun loving support, and if we are not getting sex or some kind of affection from our partner or people who are closest to us, there most likely will be an emotional or physical separation whether it be sooner or later but it is inevitable.

TRYING TO FIND THE BLESSING

The reason why God takes away from some of us what we love most is not just to punish us, but to ignite our driving force and bring our awareness to fix problems and make better what our society is lacking.

Most of us would not care about certain problems or challenges if we did not have to face them ourselves. God puts us into a position to confront and deal with problems and issues in our life so we can have compassion and awareness for others who are dealing with the same problem we had to overcome. We can help others get through their challenges because of what we personally experienced and had to go through ourselves. This process is all about caring, gaining knowledge and wisdom, and growing spiritually by expressing and sharing our love, kindness, and generosity with others.

God has a lot of compassion for us for the pain that we endure. As painful as it is, there really is a divine reason why things happen the way they do. Even when it seems like life is working against us, this is where the wisdom part of our soul is called upon to have blind faith in our darkest times, even when we don't understand why.

PURPOSE OF ANIMALS/PETS

People who are addicts, who have addictive personalities, would actually make good caregivers for the mentally challenged or animals at a shelter. Because the addict's reasoning for being an addict is that they haven't found their purpose or don't have the feeling of being loved unconditionally in their life. By them nurturing, taking care of the helpless, that feeling of love and purpose that they have to share would come right back to them through expression of appreciation from those they are helping.

Kids that are born with Autism, Down Syndrome, or other mental or physical challenges, are highly evolved souls who allow themselves to be born into this world with these health conditions. The reason why these people/souls that are born into this world putting themselves into a physically limited body isn't just for their own self growth so much, but more-so for the purpose of self growth of the parents and people who are blessed to take care of them.

Their purpose here on earth is to teach their family and care takers about being and expressing unconditional love and learning about the art of patience.

Some of the reasons why kids with disabilities that are born to certain parents and families is to actually help save them from being more destructive to themselves forcing them to have to change their selfish and/or wild ways of living.

Basically, these kids who have disabilities are making their parents and loved ones be more grounded with life, teaching them what's really real, what's important in life, rather than worrying about the little things that aren't so important or keeping them out of trouble. Going through such challenges as these, definitely helps put a whole new perspective on life.

ARE YOU IN OR ARE YOU OUT?

Definition of a healthy relationship is having chemistry, love, trust, support, communication, sharing the same values, being affectionate, and having respect for one another.

If you're in a relationship, and you find yourself trying too hard, then you're trying too hard.

Too many people want a relationship so bad that they end up doing eighty to ninety percent of the giving making their partner hardly responsible for reciprocating equally. They do most of the compromising. This is where people give away their power, making themselves feel weak and powerless to their partner. Your soul and spirit gets depleted when you do most or all of the giving. Unfortunately, too many people mistake kindness for weakness and don't show any appreciation in return because you made everything way too easy for them. You have allowed your partner to feel a sense of entitlement. Then they become disrespectful to you.

Many times, one of the partners in the relationship ends up becoming the mother or father to their other half because they feel their partner is not being responsible enough or not taking care of the responsibilities within the life circumstances of their relationship. They feel like they have to over micromanage every little thing that their partner does, they don't trust their partner to do the right thing when it's supposed to be done. It is hard to be a lover to your partner when you're looking at your partner as a child and not as your equal partner.

Here you are trying to play as a team, and your partner is playing as the selfish individual. Funny thing is, it's not all their fault! Because you have trained them in your relationship that they don't have to do much because you would do it all, or at least most of it for them. In return for all your efforts, you're looking for love, appreciation, support, and to be nurtured in return. When there are issues or problems that are concerning to you, you need to speak up and nip them in the bud rather than sweeping what's bothering you under the carpet, so to speak. Holding in your feelings, emotions, and stress without expressing your concerns can cause you to have stomach and intestinal problems. You need to speak your truth and your mind. If you can't be your true self with your partner, you're with the wrong person.

If both, you and your partner are willing to communicate and listen to what each other has to say without being defensive or attacking then your relationship has a great chance of a long term healthy survival, if that's what the both of you want. If one of you wants to work it out while the other person wants out, it's not going to work at all. Not even counseling will help. Know when the show is over, it takes two to make a healthy relationship work. If the two of you want your relationship to work out and you're just going through a rough patch, then communication and having an open mind is a major key element to great success and you will see that it will have a strong positive effect on your sex life.

If that inner child inside you is being fed with love and support then your world will be a better place to live in.

NOTHING IS REALLY A WASTE OF TIME

Ben Franklin toured universities after he was one of the people to help discover electricity. One student in the crowd asked him," How did it feel to fail over 100 times before you made your discovery? "Mr. Franklin responded by saying "I never looked at any of my experiments as a failure, I learned that each time I made a move that wasn't working, I realized that the chemistry dynamic just wasn't the way to go. I tried different ideas until I got the results I wanted. My setbacks made me become more determined. The more I tried going after something that wasn't working, the more focused I became."

There is a Chinese proverb that says, "If you get up one more time than you fall you will make it through."

God never said life was going to be easy. He said, the challenges you face, will all be worth it in the end. God will have Angels to be with you during your time here on Earth and if you need Their help or His help, all you have to do is ask.

Too many people get discouraged too easily when things don't go their way. Rather than trying new ways or ideas to make things happen or to make things better, they remain stuck like a deer in headlights and do nothing and remain either scared or frustrated.

Frequent comments that people make that limit themselves...

-"I don't want to waste time."
-"I don't want to make a mistake."
-"I don't want to waste money."
-"I don't want to make a fool of myself."

If you want something bad enough, regardless of the circumstances, you will make it happen. You make failure not an option. You can get what you want, but it might not be with the people you were originally hoping it would be with. You can get the opportunity that you are wanting, but it might not be with a project or company you are first going after. Just because you might experience some setbacks, doesn't mean you're not meant to receive.

"Your determination needs to be greater than your setbacks."

THERE IS PERFECTION IN IMPERFECTIONS

If you're specifically going after someone or something, and you're trying and trying, but it's not happening, then that just means you need to go after someone else or try a different company or a different procedure. It doesn't mean you should give up on your desires just because certain people can't appreciate your dreams. If other people don't share the same visions as you, that means they are not the ones that you should be wasting any more time with. Just go to someone else or somewhere else until you get the response or results, you're looking for. Trying over and over again with the same people or the same circumstances and keep on getting rejected!? Come on now!

They say, "The definition of insanity is someone who keeps on repeating the same thing over and over again and expecting a different result." - Albert Einstein.

I'm not saying to give up but go to different people or just change your style or your approach of how you're doing things, until you get what you want. Most of all don't ever be afraid to ask God or your Guardian Angels to send good people your way who can help you or to send you messages to guide you in the right direction.

HOW NOT TO PRAY!

You ever hear of the expression, "be careful of what you pray for?" It's so true. There is such a thing as negative prayers.

Example:
- Dear God when will they ever leave me alone?
- I don't want to grow old, alone, and poor.
- Bring it on…
- I hate when that happens, I hate when this happens.
- I hope they don't get hurt.
- I'm worried, I'm nervous.
- I can't! I can't!
- They'll be the death of me!
- Go ahead and do it. Just don't screw up.
- I give up.
- The money that I'm bringing, this is what I can afford to lose.
- Now what's going to happen, it can't get any worse.

All these words and thoughts are not going to lead you to positive results or outcomes. Acting needy, fearful, and desperate will also block you from being happy and successful.

THE RIGHT WAY TO PRAY TO ATTRACT GOOD SITUATIONS IN YOUR LIFE

- Thank you for helping me find a beautiful and healthy house that I can comfortably afford.

- Thank you for bringing my soul mate to me asap who I can happily share my life with forever and a day. The one I am attracted to as they are attracted to me/ honest / loyal / fun / financially secure / healthy / available / friendly / affectionate / generous / smart / supportive / good communicator/ etc...

-Thank you for all the beautiful blessings you have blessed me with in my lifetime!

Positive affirmations will bring you better results.

Amen!!

SUGGESTION ON HOW TO PRAY OR SPEAK FOR POSITIVE RESULTS

While speaking or saying what you want from God and the Universe out loud, it is important to also visualize the kind of results you want to see happen while saying your prayers or words. It is to your benefit to put out positive energy and believe in the words you are saying.

Here is a positive prayer to start off every day.

I call upon all my loving Guardian Angels... Thank You for intervening into my life today, bringing me peace, love, harmony, and balance. Thank You for bringing me true love and financial abundance, under healthy circumstances.

I am deserving of true love.

I am deserving of good health and happiness.

Thank You for creating the best outcomes for myself and all the people I care about
in the name of the Holy Spirit, Amen.

Here are some positive affirmations when speaking to your kids or anyone you care about when sending them off their way.

- Ok have fun! Be safe!
- I'm not worried about it, it's all good.
- Let's just fix it or take care of it.
- No problem, it's all good.

Rather than saying,
- Ok go ahead just don't screw up.

- I'm worried about you I'm nervous for you.
- Don't lose your money or cell phone!
- Don't get hurt, stay out of trouble!

Negative vibrations do not show happiness or trust in the person you are saying those words to. You're sending them off with bad juju/negative vibrations. Think positive and say positive if you want to see the best results.

SENDING GOOD ENERGY vs BAD ENERGY

When you want or would like someone to be more loving, kind, compassionate, or generous toward you, to appreciate the position you're in, in your life,

DO NOT send angry or mean thoughts to that person that you're most upset with. Why? Because, energetically, by you sending negative thoughts their way, you will be sending negative spiritual energy to keep their heart and mind hardened. They will remain resistant toward you. You will make things more difficult for yourself by experiencing the worst outcomes from that person.

If you want the people you find normally challenging for you and you want them to be more workable and agreeable with you, if you want to experience the best from them, you need to kill them with kindness. When you send others good juju/emotional good vibrations, subliminally you're melting their heart to be more pleasant while with you. For the most part, the energy that you feed to others is the same kind of energy you will experience in return from them. It might not be perfect, and it might come slow, but appreciate the improvement.

It's a shame so many people find it easier to allow fear, worry, and anger to be a part of their lives. Then they wonder why their life is so stressful. Instead, they should be expressing more love, compassion, patience, and blind faith. Why does life suck so much? Well, if you don't like the results you're getting, maybe you need to change your actions to get better results. We are a product of our environment and the people we hang out with. If you don't like your surroundings you have the right to change.

or the people who fear God or don't believe in God, never really took the time out to really get to know God.

Just because fear, evil, and negativity exist in this world and we experience very rough challenges and setbacks in our life, it doesn't mean that love, God, and our Angels don't exist. When evil presents itself, the power of your love, focus, and determination will help you override any negativity you may be facing.

Focus, believing, and patience is very important elements to the key to your happiness and success.

Stare fear in the face and you will see it was nothing more than an illusion.

WHY SOME PEOPLE HAVE A HARD TIME BELIEVING IN GOD

Just because evil exists, doesn't mean God doesn't exist. Just because there are hard challenging experiences in our life it doesn't mean God doesn't care.

By losing a loved one at birth or at an early age, does create a person to feel anger and disappointment which in return makes some people not believe in God. If someone is dealing with a terrible disease or experiences of a lot of pain for themselves or a loved one or if people are born into families with terrible family members, these experiences could make them feel that if there really was a God, then why would He allow this kind of negativity and suffering to happen? Because God created "free will," He always allows everything to happen.

That's why God has created loving Angels to help all of us through our most challenging times. Always allow yourself to call out to your Guardian Angels and ask them for whatever help you need at any time, that's what they are there for. When you ask for help, you need to ask very specifically. Only say what you do want to happen and not what you don't want to happen and with a little patience try to breathe and let go of your fears and allow things to unfold for themselves. The power of blind faith is very important to manifest what it is you want in life.

The more specific you are with your request the better outcomes you shall experience in the best way possible given the overall circumstances. Let go of your anger or fears and focus and visualize on the outcomes of what you wish to see happen.

STOP WASTING YOUR ENERGY TRYING TO CONVINCE OTHERS

When you believe in something so much, it's OK to explain your points of view or concepts freely upon any topic or issue. However, if you're using your time and energy trying to convince others how to believe, especially when their thought process is the opposite of yours, you're going to cause unnecessary arguments and create hard feelings.

Explain the knowledge you may have on a given matter. Express your opinion, your feelings, your thoughts of what's important to you, but if the other person or people are not on the same page as you, disagree with you, or simply just have a different concept than you... just agree to disagree. Wasting your energy trying to convince someone to think like you will totally drain your energy. Go ahead, bring your knowledge and info to the table. How others take it, is all in their hands. Let them have their own thoughts and if they're interested, then great! If not, let it go! Continuing trying to convince others what you believe in can zap away your energy and take away your hope or your confidence of what you believe in. When other people aren't on board with you and you keep on pushing it, it can affect the quality of your relationship with that person or people.

Everyone is entitled to think the way they want, so let it go and let them be.

Whew!

I'MMM IN HEAVEN

A lot of people say, "I want to go to Heaven, but I don't want to die."

As Woody Allen would say, "I'm not afraid of death, I just don't want to be there when it happens".

If people, on a conscious level, actually knew how beautiful Heaven really is and how powerful the love on the other side is, most of us would be checking out early.

The reason why so many people are afraid of death is because, on a conscious level, we are afraid of the unknown. The unknown always scares the hell out of us; and if we die, some of us may be thinking 'who is going to properly look after my children, or my family members, or pets if I go'. With that, most of us have that fight in us to stay alive, not just for our own sake, but for the sake of others.

THE IMPORTANCE OF BEING A GRACIOUS RECEIVER

Many of us are guilty of giving too much of ourselves to others and not allowing ourselves to receive, whether it be your children, lovers, family, people at work, friends, or strangers. There are a few reasons why we do all or most of the giving, and by our own choice, choose to receive little in return.

We've conditioned ourselves to think and feel like, 'if everyone else is happy, then I am happy'. That thought process only works for a little while. When we choose to give so much of our heart and soul away to others and not allow ourselves to receive, then what happens is that our spirit, our soul, our inner child, gets depleted. Our emotional and personal needs aren't being met. What happens is that your over kindness starts to be looked at as a weakness rather than being appreciated. The lack of appreciation by others soon turns into expectations and entitlement.

The funny thing is how the people around us look at us in that unappreciative view point and it is not all their fault! We have created and conditioned everyone to think and act the way they do towards us because we keep on accommodating most or all their expectations and not making them accountable for anything. We keep on giving them what they want even without them having to reciprocate any appreciation or responsibilities in return back to us.

WORTHINESS ISSUES

So many of us are so used to just giving and not receiving, that when most people do offer you any kind of help, your response most of the time is 'no thank you.'

- Can I help you carry something?
    - No, thank you.
- Can I get you something?
    - No, thank you.
- Can I feed you something?
    - No, thank you.
- Can I offer to pay for the bill?
    - No, thank you!!!
- Can I give you a ride?
    - No, thank you.
- Can I help you in any way?
    - No Thank you
- What can I do for you?
    - Nothing, I'm good.

You don't even realize that you keep on blocking the gift of giving from other people when they are trying to give to you. Others feel good when you accept their offer of generosity. It makes people feel bad in the moment when you deny their efforts to help you or give to you. Most of the time, when you need other people's help, they won't be around to help you when you need or ask for their help or in the way you want help because you've trained their minds to think that they don't have to help you. You've always got it taken care of by yourself.

So, let's just say I was to come to your home and I'm relaxing on your couch, you say to me,

- Hey Artie, can I get you a sandwich?

- No, thank you!

- How about some brownies? I know how much you love hot brownies!

- No, thank you, not hungry!

- Can I get you something to drink?

- No, thanks!

How frustrated would you feel if I didn't accept any of your offerings, especially while I'm in your home? Exactly! So, stop blocking other people's gift of giving to you when they are trying to make you feel good. By you receiving their offer it makes them feel good and for you as well. It's a win-win situation! And there ya go!

THE BALANCE OF GIVING

Stop putting yourself on the back burner. Most of the time, it is a blessing to give and help people, however, there is such a thing as giving too much.

Many people feel they don't have enough money, time, or resources in their life. The reason for that is not because God doesn't provide you with enough money or resources, the problem is that you give away more than what you can afford to give. Again, it's nice to help out other people, but at what cost to you?!

I look at it like this, you have your own money for necessities, that is known as 'principal,' and then you have your extra money, what's known as 'interest.' The money you have as principal, you don't give away or lend the money you need to pay your own bills or necessities of life with! By doing this, you are totally disrespecting yourself. You're taking away your own comfort zone, making yourself completely vulnerable and exhausted.

How can you help others if you're giving away your principal? You are going to end up putting yourself in the same emotional and/or financial mess as those you're trying to help, if not worse!!

Principal is the money you have and need to pay off all your bills, rent, mortgage, food, insurance, gas, utility, etc. You do not want to give your principal money away that provides for your own security and survival, otherwise you're going to be in same drama as the people you're trying to help. Interest money is the left over money you have after you pay off all your bills.

After you take care of your own financial responsibilities, if you want to then start to share a percentage of whatever left over money you may have, with other people, then that's great! Knock yourself out, help others while you're taking care of yourself. You're creating good karma for yourself and creating a win-win for those people you want to help, without killing yourself.

Yay!!

WHEN IS TOO MUCH, TOO MUCH?

Helping your kids out too much can be a major problem. There is such a thing known as being overly generous. For most families who have it pretty good, have a thought process of 'I don't want to have my kids suffer like I did'. What happens when these kinds of parents that end up giving their kid or children too much? They're taking away their children's power to become self-sufficient. When you give too much and over provide, most kids gain a sense of entitlement. When they are born into this world with you giving them so much, kissing their ass too much, they just don't know anything else. It is actually not all their fault; they are taught that their parents are always going to be there for them providing and giving to them, so they don't have to earn or do a thing to get what they want.

You're hoping to get appreciation and most of the time you hear "I want, I want!" Or "I need, I need!" They have a sense of entitlement and start to manipulate you until they get what they want. You trained them to be that way. You can try to explain to your kids all you want how hard it was for yourself or your family while growing up, but your kids won't fully get the true feeling or meaning because they've never experienced the blood, sweat, and tears it took to get to where you are or to have what you have.

You have been protecting your kids or loved ones so much from having to deal with all of life's challenges without them experiencing those challenges for themselves, you're shaping their minds to be lazy, taking away their drive to be successful and to be on top of their game. You will take away their character and ability to grow, to be self-sufficient, or to become witty enough to deal with true life situations and be responsible. Now you can understand why common sense isn't so common.

Then, you get upset with your kids or whoever you're providing for because they are mostly only thinking of themselves, or not able to think properly at all.

I believe you should teach your kids to clean up after themselves, clean dishes after dinner, throw out the garbage, and cut the lawn. If they don't want to do any chores, show them tough love, don't give them what they want. If you give your kids what they want without them pulling through on their responsibilities you're going to end up raising spoiled brats who will end up being very disrespectful to you and feeling very entitled. There are a few exceptions to the rule where there is a small percentage of children who are truly grateful and driven. Those kids were born with an old soul who naturally has that kind of understanding of appreciation.

When it comes to your relationships with other people, your goal in life is to be respected and to be liked by others, but if given only one choice between the two choices you should always choose to get respect over being liked. Being respected by others will bring you self-confidence and you will know who you are.

If you choose to continue doing nice things for those people who don't treat you nicely, you are totally disrespecting yourself. You're trying to be liked without being respected first and this will not work for you at all. You are allowing the other person to manipulate and take advantage of you. The outcome is that you'll walk away emotionally depleted and hurt. Your self-esteem will be lower than low.

Don't go chasing after other people's approval if they are not showing you some kind of appreciation or act of kindness in return.

As a parent, you should strive to be a mother or a father first and your child's friend a distant second. This way when your children become older and mature, they will still respect you more as their parent.

If you want a healthy respectful loving relationship you or your partner should not take on the mother or father role with one another.

Meaning:

If one person in the relationship is doing all the work or taking on all the responsibilities not having their partner accountable to do their fair share and one of you do most or all the work to keep things going, that's a parent/child relationship your developing, not an equal partner relationship. It's hard to remain enthusiastic or get excited emotionally or sexually towards your partner if the relationship turns into a parent/child role or even a brother/sister role. This kind of relationship creates either lots of insecurities within each other or will leave you with an emotional empty feeling and one of you are thinking "Well, I just don't trust them to take care of what needs to be done around the house or the responsibilities dealing with family matters or the finances." If you don't trust your partner or they don't trust you then what are you doing? It totally sucks when one partner is being way to controlling. If you are looking for love and respect, then stand up for yourself!! If you don't want to live your life feeling emotionally empty, then start creating balance in your relationship by becoming or making your partner more responsible.

WHAT ABOUT YOUR GOALS AND HAPPINESS?

How long have you been choosing other people's happiness over yours?

How long have you been saying, 'as long as they're happy, then I'm happy?'

How much longer are you going to keep on putting your heart and desires on the back burner?

Don't ever stop being kind and loving to yourself while you're being Mother Theresa to everyone else. Start creating time out for you to enjoy life with no guilt. Being that you're always busy 24/7 taking care of everyone else's needs and all other responsibilities, take a half day or evening, or even a full day out, just for yourself. Whether it is once a week or at least once every two weeks but give yourself something fun and pleasant to look forward to.

A big mistake that parents make is that once they start having kids, they put their relationship and themselves on the back burner. Mommy and daddy have a tendency to stop treating each other like boyfriend and girlfriend. They stop going out with each other, stop being as intimate, stop going out with their friends. A couple times a week or every other week, it is important to keep that love connection and communication going; otherwise, you are going to start drifting apart.

Mommy starts getting more into the mommy stage and dad begins to get more lost in his job, pleasures, or with other people to fulfill his own personal needs. When two people stop nurturing each other, the next move is to drift toward other people outside their own relationship to fulfill that emotional void that their partner isn't filling. Those people who actually don't drift off and stay obedient, remain suppressing their feelings of anger and resentment within themselves, turning into an unhappy person.

Make time for yourself and with your partner in life and connect with doing fun things you enjoy.

You know when you're with the right person? When you enjoy each other's company, when you're willingly and happily having good conversations with each other, you enjoy seeing and kissing each other, you love making love with one another. When you both can say, "I love you," to each other, and mean it, then you know you got a good thing, but if you don't have that, then it's time to either make things better with each other or go your separate ways.

Too many people remain content in their relationship and end up falling into a rut or a routine and wonder when are things going to change, when is something special going to happen? But it never does for a lot of people. They don't make the effort with each other to do different things or to do special things for their partner or better yet, yourself. Having a quality relationship takes two people to make an effort to make magic happen.

MONEY IS A BLESSING NOT A CURSE

For anyone to say money is the root of all evil are the ones who don't have it. Money isn't the root of evil, people are. Similarly, when people say that guns kill people. The truth is, guns are innocent it is just an object lying there. It is the person loading it, the person pulling its trigger that makes a gun dangerous. Just like everything else in life, it is about the intention behind the action that makes something either right or wrong.

In today's society, we need money like we need air. Money can give you a quality of life. When you have financial freedom in your life it gives you a strong sense of security, it gives you the ability to choose freely, it is there to pay off all your personal bills, you can enjoy going on trips and doing fun things.

It's true; money can't buy you emotional happiness. Emotional happiness comes from within you not from material gains. People who find happiness in material gains, a lot of that happiness is shallow and is usually short lived. Like everything else in life, it is all about balance. When you respect the energy of money, money will treat you very well. The true happiness of having money isn't just based on your own security and buying things, the happiness of financial freedom comes by making a difference in other people's lives by sharing some of what you have with those who are less fortunate and need it.

Making a positive difference in other people's lives by sharing some of what you have with them is a major blessing. When you manifest and respect the energy of money, it will bring you peace of mind. If you disrespect money by stealing it or using it to manipulate people, to get others to do what you want, basically bribery with bad intentions, Karma will bite you in the ass for trying to take advantage of people. You should never feel guilty for having the ability to make or have a lot of money.

Having plenty or enough money is a blessing....and as a reminder, it is very important to be grateful for everything you have and not just money.

What happens to people when they have plenty of money and share very little or don't share at all? They can get emotionally sick. They will always worry; will I have enough? Who is trying to steal from me? Who are my true friends? Is my partner with me for me, or for my money? Unfortunately, people look at money as their God, and not as a beauty of energy as it is meant to be.

In today's society, money is more like food. When you have so much food on the table and you try to eat it all by yourself, you can get very sick or have a terrible stomachache trying to hoard It all for yourself. When you eat just enough to satisfy yourself and you share the rest with everyone else at the table, your body and soul are feeling very comfortable when you take care of yourself along with others.

It is all about balance, because on the flip side, If you feed everyone else and not yourself, that's not good either. There is no reason for you to just feed everyone else at the table and not properly nourish yourself.

People do the same thing with their money. You have a decent amount of it but have a tendency to give too much away to others and then don't have enough to take care of your own financial needs and responsibilities. You put the value of other's needs above your own making their problems yours as well. You shouldn't do that to yourself. How can you be in a strong position in life if you're giving too much of your power away to other people?

Learn to respect the energy and balance of your money staying within your means and you will be emotionally a much more confident and comfortable person without all the stress of finances.

If money was really that evil, the Churches and Temples would not be asking their members to give them lots if it!

MONEY

Is money really the root to all evil or is it the ego of the mind where the evil comes from? The energy of money can literally be one of your best friends. It's a strong ally when you respect the energy of what it is. It's all about balance.

It has been said many times that money is the root to all evil. When you have enough money and you respect it, it gives you security and pays for the responsibilities in your life, such as education, food, clothes, rent, mortgage, utilities, car, phone, gas, insurance, etc. It helps you buy luxuries such as TVs, radio, vacations, jewelry, boats, cars, motorcycles, entertainment, pleasures, etc.

We have heard sermons by Priests, Ministers, and Rabbi's telling us that money is the root to all evil and that we should not ask God for it, we are being selfish, greedy, that it is a sin, yet they are the ones always asking for our donations. My attitude is, "Sorry Father, sorry Rabbi, I would love to give you large donations, but I just heard your sermon and you just said, money is the root to all evil and we shouldn't ask God for money because that would be greedy, that it's a sin asking God for money." I don't want to corrupt your Church or Temple so I'm not going to share my evil money with you. I don't care what anyone might say, but, having way more than enough money is much better than not having enough money at all.

Money is definitely not everything in life, and money doesn't guarantee you or anyone else happiness. It can't buy you true love, it might buy you the illusion of love, but that's for people who are looking to be in a relationship for security reasons more than love itself. It is extremely important to have enough of it to give you the peace of mind and security we all need and want. It gives us freedom of choice when we have it. It's important to respect the energy of money. According to the amount you have, it will give you a certain quality of life.

What is considered to be enough money? It all depends on what your needs are. Everyone's needs are different. Some people don't need as much money as others according to their lifestyle and choices in life. As for other people, it makes no difference how much money they make it's still never enough because of their insecurities, spending habits, and their desires that are much greater than what they make. This tends to put people under very stressful times, when their bills or spending habits are more than what they make.

The blessings and importance of having extra money in your possession is that you can help others who are less fortunate. When you share a percentage of your money, that you can afford to give away, you're opening up the energy of the Universe for more money to come and find its way to you. There is such a thing called balance, meaning you don't want to give so much of your money away to others that you leave yourself stranded. You are not being fair to yourself if you are giving your friends and/or family members too much where you leave yourself struggling to pay your own bills.

Many times, God gives you the means to have enough money in your life, to pay all your bills and take care of your responsibilities. The mistake many of us make is that we have a habit of giving away too much money to others that we personally can't afford and need for ourselves to survive. Now, by you being overly generous, you just put yourself in the same crappy situation of the person or people you were just trying to help. You say "but they need it!" And I'm saying to you, "Yeah, but so do you!" It is nice to help others out but not at the emotional expense of your security and sanity. It's always nice to be kind to others but just don't give away more than you can comfortably afford to give.

My friend, who is a very generous person, once said to me... "I don't mind helping out other people, but I'll be damned if I'm going to sink my ship while trying to save someone else's."

I will always remember those words.

There's also the greed factor, money can change people. When people who are blessed to have way more money than they possibly need, but they choose not to share a percentage of it with others, they want to hoard and keep it all for themselves, that's greedy. When profits are being divided among people appointed in a will or a business agreement and someone is trying to keep more than their fair share, now that's being greedy. There are people who have more money than others and think they are better than everyone else, that's being arrogant.

When you appreciate and respect the energy of money, it really is a beautiful thing. When you have the ability to improve the quality of someone else's life, money is like fire, fire is only evil when you disrespect it. Money and fire can be your friend or your enemy it all comes down to respecting the energy of what you're dealing with, given the circumstances.

Fire keeps us warm, cooks our food, and gives us light. When disrespected, it can burn down nature, our homes, and ourselves. This isn't about being fearful of fire or anything; it all comes down to respect.

Money: When you consistently give away money, specifically to other people, a lot of times you enable them and condition them to become dependent on you. Their appreciation, with time turns into expectations and entitlement.

When you spot help someone once in a while, it keeps up their appreciation. Constantly helping someone definitely turns the person's mindset on the receiving end, into entitlement and builds expectations. Many times, we discover who our true friends are by those who pay us back the money we lend to them. If they don't pay it back, unfortunately it just cost you that much to discover that they really aren't your friend or to discover they don't have integrity. They were just using you rather than being genuine. The blessing is, you still get rewarded and score big points for your generosity in the eyes of the Lord.

When it comes to donating: There are times you will donate money or some kind of resource to others and it never reaches the people or purpose it was intended for. Whether it was mismanaged or stolen, however according to the eyes of the Lord, you still get full credit, spiritually, because you had best of intentions when donating. The people who mismanaged or stole your donations are the ones who are going to spiritually suffer; the emotional quality of one's life is going to go way down.

If you're going to donate loose change to people who live out in the street, don't worry how they choose to spend it. Your intentions are that they hopefully will use it towards buying food or a place for shelter. However, if the person who receives that money chooses to buy drugs or alcohol, is it OK? Yes, I said it's OK! Why? If that is their choice, then that's their choice. When they buy alcohol or drugs, they feed themselves emotionally, to satisfy their moment. Even though we wish for them to buy food with our donation and feed their body, it is still their choice. Don't judge them as you don't know their story or why they do what they do. You're not in their position, Thank God!

Amen!

RELATIONSHIP / SPIRITUALITY / RATED X

The what if factor.

You're in a personal relationship and you want sex, but your partner doesn't want to have sex, what should the sexless person do?! There's a very strong possibility that the person who is not receiving sex is going to either end up cheating on their partner or leaving the relationship. Why should the person be wanting sex to starve themselves emotionally, wanting that feeling, when their partner is not into it? It's a natural human feeling of desire wanting to be nurtured in the emotional and physical sense of having sex.

It blows me away when someone provides for the family and/or partner and in return they are unfortunately being emotionally or sexually deprived by their partner. That situation usually spells out loudly that there is going to be cheating on the horizon at some point within that relationship or that relationship has a time limit on it for it to end. Why on God's green Earth, should the person be wanting sex to go without it if their partner isn't into it?

The temporary savior and solution from stepping out of the relationship is masturbation. If you can't get what you want from your partner, sexually, and you don't want to cheat, meaning (stepping out of your relationship for sex) then masturbation will go a long way to give you that sexual pleasure of release.

The comedian Woody Allen said it best, "Having sex is like the card game of bridge. If you don't have a good partner, you'd better have a good hand"

I don't care what any Religion says, masturbation is not a sin! It is a natural, healthy, emotional, and physical release for the human body and spirit. We are able to have and enjoy the pleasure of that experience. The jack ass who created the thought process that some clergy people can't experience the pleasures of sex while serving God was incredibly arrogant and naïve.

God created the pleasures of sex for us to enjoy and not just for procreation purposes. This is one of the best gifts God has given to mankind. Having sex is one of the beautiful ways to express love with the one you love. However, just because you have sex with someone doesn't mean it's about love or romance. It can be just a personal magnetism kind of chemistry that two people have for one another, where they have that physical chemistry and attraction just to enjoy the wonderful pleasure of having great sex. Having sex with someone could simply be just enjoying the pleasure of having sex without being in love. Like I said before, sometimes the human body or the emotions of the mind is simply wanting to enjoy the experience of that great feeling with no strings attached. Some people are not capable to leave emotions out of it, but that's something very important between the two partners should discuss so they have an understanding about one another before they start to have a sexual relationship.

Of course, there is a time and place for everything. If you have an urge for sexual release, do it in private, not in public where others can see or hear you. You should have respect for other people when you are doing something that is very personal. Do it in a private place where no one will feel offended or bothered by your personal actions of pleasure.

Releasing yourself to have an orgasm can be such an incredible high if you can't do it with a partner, its 100% OK to experience that pleasure of sexually taking care of yourself. There's nothing wrong with taking care of yourself sexually if you don't have a partner to please you in that way.

If you are looking for a long-term relationship with someone, you do not want to sleep with them right away. You want to build on the emotional aspect of your relationship first and get to know each other really well and then celebrate it by making love. It's like putting icing on the cake after you have finished making the base foundation of the cake itself. The cake is the relationship and the icing on it is the sex part, sweet and tasty. Lol.

The difference between making love and having just sex: Making love is when you're emotionally invested while having sex. Having sex without emotions is just the physical action of two or more people getting together just for pleasure with little or no emotions invested on either party's part. There are people who get together just to have sex, a relationship better known as "friends with benefits." That kind of relationship can work as long as both parties are on the same emotional page with one another.

I feel it is perfectly okay to have sex with somebody right away if you want to just have the pleasure of having sex with someone without any emotional, long-term commitment, even if you just met for the first or second time. If it's just going to be about just having sex with no emotional commitment to each other, and you accept one another for who you are, unconditionally, with no strings attached, then go for it! Sometimes we just have that urge within us that we want to have fun and wild sex with no strings attached, to get release, that desire that's burning inside of us.

Those who do not experience having sex on any level, many times, can create internal frustrations and tensions within their body and mind. Sexually frustrated people often become angry or depressed. Some people simply enjoy the pleasure of having sex on a physical level, and that's fine, too. However, when you have deep feelings for someone and you're having sex with that person, that orgasmic feeling is like being on a rocket-ship, flying through the Milky Way. If you ever find that partner, where the two of you have that deep spiritual emotional connection with one another, your sex life should be off the charts. Consider yourselves truly blessed.

With some people, the sex is so good that when they finish, even the neighbors need a cigarette.

Just like money, sex isn't everything in a relationship, but it sure is very important to have and express one's love.

Amen!

THE BENEFITS OF FORGIVENESS

It's important to be as forgiving as possible. Forgiveness is the most powerful action and ingredient to heal oneself. When you forgive someone, you are releasing anger/resentment and tension out of your body and soul.

Here are some benefits of forgiving someone as well as being forgiving toward yourself:

- You'll be a kinder person.
- You won't be on edge as often.
- You'll sleep better.
- Your physical body can heal itself better from any sickness.
- Your prosperity can grow faster and easier.

Why? Because you're releasing all of the negative emotional dead weight energy out of your body and out of your system. Your outlook on life will be clearer and better all around. Or you can choose to remain bitter and angry and hold yourself back. That choice is yours.

TRUST AND LOVE

Trust is like a tree; it takes years to grow and a moment to cut it down.

When it comes to any relationship, trust and respect is just as important as love. Trust isn't just about being faithful; it's also about being trustworthy.

Meaning:

- Do they do what they say they're going to do?
- Show up when they say they're going to show up?
- Not taking more than what was agreed upon.
- Doing a good job according to your expectations.
- Not stealing from you or anybody else.
- Are their words meeting up according to their actions?

If someone is not respecting your feelings, that is a form of lack of trust. If someone is purposely holding back information from you, that is lack of trust. If they are physically or emotionally being abusive that is a lack of trust. Now it's up to you if you choose to allow yourself to hold on to a relationship like this. If someone in your life, whether it be friend or lover, possesses most of these qualities, then they are not your friend or true love. It is time for you to stand up and start respecting yourself. That is where the self-forgiveness comes in.

People, who choose to stay in any type of relationship that has no trust or respect, deserve what they get from the other person. Their partner is just being who they are, and the person being abused chooses to stay in the relationship to be their partner's pincushion and take on the pain that their partner gives them.

Again!! If your gut is telling you something doesn't feel right pertaining to whom you are spending your time with then it's time to create harmony and balance in your life. Start making the necessary changes that will please you, bringing you to a safe and healthy environment where you belong.

When are things going to change and get better in your life? When you change!

If not now, then when?

TOUGH LOVE

If you give too much to others, you make them weak. Appreciation turns into expectations. You take away their character and strength to figure things out for themselves. You take away their ability to be self-sufficient.

Showing someone tough love is your best answer.

Like the old saying goes, "Give a man a fish, and you'll feed him for a day. Teach a man how to fish, and you've fed him for a lifetime."

Instant gratification is a pleasant experience for the moment, but the feelings and appreciation many times doesn't last long. Stop putting band aids on situations that are only temporarily satisfying the moment. Do the right thing; go after the cure to make the situation permanently better.

Metaphorically speaking, too many times people give their loved one's stronger crutches or better wheelchairs to help them get by better for the moment. That's a nice band aid for the now, but rather than giving them nicer tools to satisfy the moment, why don't you help them build their muscles so they can stand and walk on their own two feet, so they won't need the crutches or the wheelchair anymore that you provided them with.

BEING A KIND SOUL AND DOING THE RIGHT THING

Being a good person isn't just about going to Church or Temple every week or every holiday, it isn't just about your prayers. It is about being compassionate and forgiving towards your fellow man. It is about the intentions and kindness behind your actions. That's what means the most to God.

When you say your prayers, do you feel the words and true meaning of what you are saying or are you just going through the motions because you were taught that's the right thing to do?

When you ask God for his forgiveness, are you able to stop doing those specific actions of whatever it is that you're asking His forgiveness for? What good is it? How much power do your words hold when or if you are consciously aware of your wrongdoings and you keep repeating the same negative words or actions over and over again? When you say your prayers, but you continue to think or act negatively, don't you realize you're being very hypocritical?

When you feel the words of your prayers as you are saying them or thinking them, and you agree to continue making the positive changes toward being loving and kind, then you are actually walking your talk, because you're expressing yourself with the emotional feelings of your heart. Under these conditions, you will start to experience more blessings in your life.

OPEN YOUR HEART AND WORK YOUR WILL

When it comes to attracting anything into your life, it's not about just being a nice person, It all comes down to how strong your will is for you to make things happen. How bad do you want it?

You want to know how unconditional God's love is for us?

There are people who say they are angry with God. There are people who say that they don't believe in God...and ya know what? God will still give everyone his love, the necessities and resources of life to live and still allow the non-believers to have the pleasures of life just like everyone else. However, just because someone has a certain amount of nice material things in their life, doesn't mean their heart and soul is fulfilled and happy if there isn't that sense of appreciation or presence of someone in their life to share their glory with.

If you don't allow love to enter into your life, if you don't share love with others, all your money and possessions can kind of carry a feeling of emptiness. The things you attain in life can become meaningless. This is why there are a good amount of people who have so much material things in their life, but still aren't happy. They lack love for themselves or having that special someone in their life to share their good fortunes with. They remain bitter or fearful of other people who are jealous or trying to take what they have away from them. By showing appreciation or acknowledgment to God for all the Blessings in your life and sharing your glory with others, your life will be filled with happiness and continue to prosper.

WE ALL HAVE GUARDIAN ANGELS

Many times, people ask me, "Artie, do I have Guardian Angels around me? Who are my Angels?"

The answer is always, YES!

Every person born has at least two Guardian Angels with them 24/7. If you need your Angels' help, all you have to do is speak out loud and ask for their help. Your Angels will help you find what you're looking for or get what you need to help improve matters for you. When you ask for their help, you have to be able to let go of control of your situation and just let things fall into place on their own.

If you're going after a situation like to improve your education or pursuing certain accomplishments, you still have to do the work to get things done to get ahead. Your Angels will work with you behind the scenes, to help make your situation more pleasant or serve as your assistants to help you get what it is you're trying to accomplish. Even if you do not see immediate results, sooner or later you will. When you let go of control, situations might not be going according to your original plan, but in the end, the grand scheme of things, everything will end up happening in a way that is best for your overall good.

You can't think like my 6 year old daughter once did...

I told her she has Guardian Angels around her that will help her out in life, all you have to do is ask for their help. One day, when I asked her if she had done her homework, she responded with "No, I wasn't in the mood to do it, so I asked my Angels to do it for me!" Needless to say, I had to re-explain to her how that Angel thing works. Lol

HOW BAD DO YOU WANT IT?

- What are you willing to do, to do what it takes, to get what it is you say you want?

How bad do you want it?

- What are you willing to sacrifice to get the results you are looking for?

How bad do you want it?

- What kind of risk are you willing to take to get what you want?

How bad do you want it?

- If at first you don't succeed, how determined are you to rework what you started and improve what you got?

How bad do you want it?

- What happens if the people around you don't support your visions, but you really know in your heart that you're right, or the move you're trying to make will make you happy?

How bad do you want it?

God places no limitations on you, you place the limitations on yourself. How determined are you to go after what you want? God supports the direction of your choice. Your will is God's will. It isn't just what God wants for you, it's how strong your will is to make things happen.

- Fear or self-pity won't buy you squat. Fear and self-pity will keep you stuck, limited, and very unhappy.

How bad do you want it?

- What is the "it"? It's your success and/or your happiness. So, what are you willing to do and go through to get it?

How bad do you want it?

HOW TO COMMUNICATE TO YOUR LOVE PARTNER

It is so important to know how to talk to your partner, to be able to sustain harmony in your relationship. Too many times people sweep their bothered emotions or feelings under the carpet in order to avoid confrontation. People have a tendency to hold back on their negative feelings toward their partner, friends, co-workers, or family members. People have a tendency of not speaking their truth, so they don't 'rock the boat,' to keep everything nice and balanced for everybody else, but not themselves.

Meanwhile, your inner child is being hurt, your feelings are not being cared about or comforted. Anger, disappointment, and resentment start to build up inside you. Finally, after holding it in for so long you snap!! Your voice gets loud; your partner becomes defensive and doesn't hear what you have to say. They will only come back at you with their point of view to say what they have to say, not taking your point of view into consideration, if at all only very little. Your ego will project the anger and disappointment through the tone or volume of your voice, or curse them out, out of frustration. At that point, your ego is expressing itself strictly out of anger and not from your emotional soulful side. When you yell and scream, you've lost all control of yourself. The calmer you are during any kind of discussion, the more control you have. You calmly want to express your feelings from your soulful side to the other person that hurt you and let them know how they made you feel. Share your pain with them so they can appreciate the course of their actions or words, how they made you feel. By doing so, you are honoring yourself. You are respecting that inner child inside you because your true feelings are now being heard.

HOW TO COMMUNICATE TO YOUR LOVE PARTNER

When you tell someone something that's important to you or if something is bothering you, you would be more effective if you started off your conversation by saying something like,

- "I would appreciate it if..."
- "I don't appreciate it when..."

...if your partner or some other person is not being mindful of you, you can start off by saying or using any one of these phrases,

- "Would you mind if..."
- "Can you please..."
- "It bothers me when you..."
- "It hurts my feelings when you..."

Timing is very important, knowing when to say and what to say to your partner or any other person when you need to express your true feelings. You want to figure out when that person you need to speak with is going to be most receptive to hearing what you have to say. Not only is timing important, but also the style of your delivery. It isn't always what you say, but how you say it that will determine how well people will listen and respond to you, whether it be with a positive tone or negative. It's like being a good standup comic or storyteller, it's all in the timing and delivery on how well people understand and take in what you have to say.

LIVING IN THE WORLD OF "WHAT IFs"

Jumping to conclusions and creating hypothetical negative thoughts and assumptions can make you sick and ruin your relationships.

What if this happens, what if that happens? One of the worst things you can do to yourself and those who are a part of your life, is to assume the worst outcomes and always talk and think negative. Living your life with constant intensity, consciously or subconsciously, thinking negative thoughts, worries, always walking around being or acting nervous, waiting for some kind of bad news to arise even when there's nothing wrong you're only going to make all the feelings and circumstances around you worse and unpleasant.

Negative thoughts + Negative actions = Create negative results.

Positive thoughts + Positive actions = Create positive results.

Not only are you making yourself a nervous wreck, but all the people around you as well. By being high strung, high anxiety, and with constant nervous energy, you will never have peace of mind or a harmonious lifestyle, not to mention creating the relationships around you not to be pleasant at all.

Trying to keep happy when hanging out with negative people is like trying to fly a kite without any wind. Enthusiasm is contagious. Energy is contagious. What you create, you can expect in return. If you want nice you need to be nice.

CAN I HELP YOU? Or not...

You can't help someone be healed if they don't want to heal. You can't make someone happy if they don't have happiness within themselves.

The best thing to do under those circumstances is to be there for them unconditionally and sometimes just be a good listener. Listen to what they have to say and just allow them to speak their mind without judging them. In your own loving way let them know you care. Let them know they're loved and not alone. It will still be up to them to do the work and/or accept help. If they don't accept or want anyone's help, you need to just let them be so they can either figure it out for themselves or just deal with their own choices in life. The more you try to help someone who does not want to be helped, the more emotional pain you are going to endure. It's hard not to feel guilty when you love someone so much that you want to help, yet they are not willing to help themselves. Their choices and problems can and will devastate you if you don't protect yourself while allowing yourself to still be involved with them.

The best thing to do is let go of control and put your prayers out there on their behalf. Allow God and the Angels to assist them, they have to be ready and willing to open up their heart and let the sunshine in. Some things are simply out of your hands.

If you're going to allow someone to live with you while they're doing drugs, you can expect to be lied to and stolen from, and most likely you'll be doing a lot of arguing. Just protect yourself. Hide your valuables! Keep your bedroom doors locked! Protect yourself!

The secret to help someone stay off of drugs, you need to help them with a future vision. Create a beautiful dream for them to look forward to once they are off of drugs.

Help them think:

70

- What kind of exciting job or career would you like to go after once you are clean from drugs?

-What do you find exciting in life that you want to accomplish once you are clean?

- What do you want to buy?

- Where do you want to go?

Help them create positive thoughts to give them something to look forward to once they are clean. Whatever makes them happy, what do they want to achieve? Where do they want to go, where do they want to travel to?

If the people who become clean after their program have no goals or dreams to look forward to once they are clean, they think, "Ok, what's next?"

If there's nothing to look forward to after they get clean, chances are they are going to relapse.

Alright, I'm clean...now what? Create the goal and the dream to keep them clean.

THEY HEAR YOU

If you find yourself having major problems with your health/wealth or in your personal relationship or relationship with others, now would be a good time to develop a closer relationship with God and your Guardian Angels. They will give you more love, support, and comfort than you could ever imagine.

P.S. Talk to them, they're really good listeners.

Feeling stressed out these days?

- Go to a beach or a lake.
- Take a walk-in nature.
- Go to a park.
- Watch and feed the birds outside.
- Play with your pets.
- Go to the gym.
- Call an old friend who you really like and/or love.
- Go biking.

...the list goes on, just do whatever makes you happy!

SELF RESPECT

If you notice people will treat you the same way you treat yourself. Your partner will treat you in one way while Your friends treat you one way, your coworkers treat you a different way, and your family members treat you another way. Why? It is all in how you act or how you handle yourself when you're in the company of certain people or according to what circumstances that you're in at any given moment.

If people aren't treating you the way you want or deserve, there are two things you can do. You can speak up for yourself and let them know how you feel, set boundaries by setting the tone for others of what's cool or not cool by your standards or you can just cut them out of your life altogether if they are not willing to appreciate or respect you for how you wish to be accepted and/or appreciated, just move on.

If you're chasing the approval of others that means you aren't approving of yourself. I used to walk into a room wondering if people will accept me for who I am. Now I walk into the room thinking, will I accept them?

If you don't like who you are, then make the necessary changes of how you wish to be. You can't just talk about it and not make the necessary changes then expect people to treat you in the way that you want or just expect things to get better on their own. You need to act in a certain way and be willing to express yourself in the manner of how you wish to be perceived by the public. If you do not like how you're being treated by someone you have to be willing to make the necessary changes for yourself so you can be taken seriously by others in the way that you wish to be perceived. People will treat you according to how you act and the way you handle yourself. If you want to be taken seriously or treated with respect, you can't come off as someone who is a pushover or a jackass. You need to create boundaries of what's acceptable to you and what is not. If you are a pushover to other people, then you will not be respected or appreciated In the way that you want to be. You cannot come off as acting lazy, needy, flighty, or way too silly, unless you purposely want to come off as a goofball, then that's a different story if that's what your intentions are just to be playful. There is a time to be serious and there's a time to be playful it all depends on what the circumstances call for in that given moment.

Talk is cheap, baby. You want to be treated differently? Then you have to be willing to make some changes on how you handle yourself and start to do something about it.

Where can you begin?

You can start by focusing on self-love and self-respect.

TILL DEATH DO YOU PART

A lot of people really do mean what they say, in the moment. It doesn't mean those feelings will remain forever.

When two people are married and the words are said, "Till death do us part, we shall be together," according to religion and the physical world, the words mean until one of you physically die and you must stick and stay together no matter what.

The true meaning of those words, "Until death do us part," according to the spiritual world is, we shall always remain together unless one of our hearts was to die in the relationship, whether it be physically or emotionally. "Till death do us part."

God wants nothing more than for you to be happy. No one can make a guarantee on how people will feel about each other as the years move on and our lives grow and change.

Where the two of you are in the beginning of your relationship, the chemistry between the two of you is assumingly great, the sex is good, you accept and love each other for how the both of you are, at least in the now. That's awesome! As life starts to evolve, moving forward, life will naturally start to change while new experiences come your way, for the both of you. You'll start to meet new people at work or meet new friends while you're out and about doing your thing in life or when kids come into the picture, your relationship and your values may differ on how to raise them. Your interests may change. One of you in your relationship wants more sex than the other, one's expectations or desires for wanting more intimacy can very well be stronger than your partner's or vice versa.

If one person's needs aren't being met in the relationship, that can lead someone into having an affair, not always, but mostly. If financial issues arise, many times the stress of the financial burden puts an end to a relationship. Your expectations of where you thought you would be can become emotionally draining when you're always worried about money. Money isn't everything in life, just like sex or intimacy, but it sure is very important to have in a relationship or in one's life.

God forbid, one of you get sick or debilitated, one person wants to go and do things and the other person can't because of their health issues, frustrations and resentment can kick in. For our own selfish reasons, 'why should I be limited just because my partner is? I will help my partner as much as I possibly can, but do I need to limit my personal desires as well just because my partner is limited?' There are many people who are devoted to their partner so much that they are willing to limit what they do with their life, even if it means spending a lot of time with their partner so that they are not alone. That's great! That's commitment of true love, but again, you should allow yourself to do your own thing. Do what you want or need to do as long as your partner is physically taken care of, then do your thing.

What happens if one of you has trust issues and you or your partner becomes very controlling? Jealousy can have you feeling like you're always walking on eggshells just because you're afraid of what your partner may think, say, or do. You may very well have a hard time just being yourself, walking around nervous as if you're doing something wrong, even though you may not be.

Your partner didn't start off that way when you first got together or got married, but over time, they became insecure. They don't trust you or anyone else, well maybe a few people, but not many. Rather than enjoying your relationship, you start to feel like a prisoner. For you and your partner it should be a pleasure to share time with each other and not having an emotional feeling of an anchor or a killjoy of your happiness and dreams.

If the two of you really love each other and you both want to stay together, it would be a great idea to seek out a good counselor. Find someone that you both like so that you get an outside opinion from a third party that is not emotionally connected to any of you. That way, you could hopefully get to a place where you'll be able to see each other's point of view and make some compromises to work things out. If one of you wants to see a counselor but the other person is not willing to go with you or vice versa, that tells you that they are not willing to make your relationship better and they are no longer interested in staying in it to be happy or in it at all. Under these circumstances, you should strongly consider moving on with your life without your partner. You can find someone else who is more suited for you at this point in your life. It's very difficult to stay in a relationship where there is at least one person who is not willing to be a good communicator, not willing to share their feelings and thoughts with you. That can definitely make one person, if not two people, within the same relationship feel very alone. Hence the words "Until death do us part..."

IT'S IN GOD'S HANDS

Not everything in life is meant to be fixed, cured, or perfect, at least according to our personal expectations. There's nothing you can do about it. It is what it is. Sometimes it is simply about letting go of control and coming to a place of acceptance.

You may need time to mourn a situation and regroup your thoughts so you could move on to new beginnings in your life.

Prayers and positive thoughts will help you overcome any setbacks.

It is important to believe.

BLESSINGS AND ACCEPTANCE

God knew life was going to be a challenging journey for you. So, to help make it easier or as pleasant as possible, He gave us the gifts of love, music, food, laughter, dance, entertainment, technology, beauty of nature, pets, and all our Angels to help us enjoy and get through all our challenging times.

If anyone has discovered how to change the past from any past mistake or regrets, please let us all know how to go about it.

The healthy attitude is to accept what has happened and learn from it. Just because you accept it doesn't mean you have to like it. You should stop beating yourself up about past events and experiences that you cannot change. You have no control over what has happened in the past. Learn from your past, make healthier choices that will benefit you and others and allow yourself to move on so you can start to heal and grow.

BEING STRUCTURED AND ORGANIZED IS KEY TO SUCCESS

It is important to be organized if you wish to have peace of mind and success. There are a lot of us who just wing things in the moment without pre-planning anything. We just go and do. Many times it works for us, but what happens when things don't go your way and you're trying really hard to make things happen? Meanwhile, you're under crunch time and you can't find what you're looking for while juggling many situations and multi-tasking. The stress is on!

- Where did I put those papers?
- Where did I put those keys?
- Who was I supposed to call?
- I know I had an appointment with someone...where, who, and when?
- Oh darn, I'm running behind!
- I'm always running late.

It is important to perform well while under pressure. When you have a schedule book or some kind of a planner, all you have to do is look down in your notes, so you know what's what... who's who... and where you're supposed to be. This is what's known as being organized.

Trying to remember everything in your head, you will be blocked in your mind when dealing with stressful moments. This stress will cause you to forget all the things you need or want to do. That's why it is important to have a game plan/plan of attack to get things done, whether it be short term or long-term goals.

Being organized and having things written down that need to be done, will put you in control, give you power, make you feel confident, and most of all give you peace of mind. Having everything in place and having control will increase your odds of being happy and becoming much more successful.

PROOF THAT SANTA CLAUS DOES EXIST

The real Santa Claus was a Dutch Monk known as Saint Nicholas.

Saint Nicholas was a very wealthy and generous man who was born in Turkey, approximately 280 A.D. He was/is a patron Saint who watched over children and sailors. When he was alive, he did what he could to help not only children, but the poor as well. He was the most beloved Saint throughout all of Europe because of his generosity.

Another man by the name of Clement Clarke Moore, who claimed authorship in 1837, of a poem that was first anonymously published in 1823, called "'Twas the night before Christmas." That poem inspired Thomas Nast to create the jolly image of Saint Nick, who we know as "Santa Claus."

Just like a lot of us can feel the love and energy of our own loved ones who have passed away (in spirit), the love and kindness we share with others during the holiday season is inspired by the soul and spirit of Saint Nick, also known as Santa. That's why Santa can be everywhere, because love and kindness is shared by all.

Just like the sign of the cross that represents Jesus, the image of Santa Claus represents Saint Nicholas.

- Does Saint Nick really exist?

- Heck, Yeah!

- Does Santa Claus really exist?

- Heck, Yeah!

GOD, WHY AM I HERE?

The reason you are here, on Earth, is so that you can spiritually grow.

Before you were born, you were hanging out in Heaven with your Angels and spirit guides and they helped you make some major decisions in your life, but you have the ultimate say on your experiences coming into this world. Did you know that you were the one who picked your parents? You are the one who picks how you are going to die and when (with the exception of suicide, that is never part of the plan.) You are the one who picks the major challenges in your life and you know in advance most of the people you are going to experience having in your life.

Now, a lot of you will say,

- "Why the hell would I pick alcoholic parents or partners in my life?"

- "Why would I pick poverty or sickness?"

- "Why would I choose a life where I lose someone at an early age?"

- "Why would I pick a life with such emotional problems?"

- "Why would I pick a life with such health issues?"

...And the reason why is, so that you can spiritually grow.

We come here to learn about and experience unconditional love, blind faith, patience, forgiveness, respect, and how to have compassion. The only way to learn about these emotional experiences is to deal with life's challenges.

Those who choose to remain bitter and not handle your challenges gracefully or humbly, you're going to have to re-live your experiences all over again in the next lifetime.

...and, oh yes, there is reincarnation! Whether you believe it or not. This lifetime is not your one shot deal. We all have many lifetimes to deal with, dealing with different circumstances and situations in our lives, we are here to learn and grow from our experiences. Life is like a play; we put on different costumes and play different characters according to the different plays that we're in.

I explain to people that to grow spiritually is a lot like trying to become a good boxer, you have to learn to take a good ass kicking if you want to become a better boxer.

If life was always perfect, there would be no reason for you to be here. That's what vacations and tropical islands are for, to take a break from the havoc of your daily life and responsibilities. When you are away on vacation in paradise, that's perfection. That's Heaven on Earth.

TRUE LOVE

There are different variations of true love.

- True love is when you see someone for who they are and regardless of their flaws, you just love them with all your heart.

- True love is when you can see the good and potential in someone, even if they can't see it for themself.

- True love is, wanting to hear or see someone everyday of your life.

- True love is, missing someone when they are not with you.

- True love is, believing not only in God's existence, but knowing the unconditional love, patience, and compassion he has for you.

- True love is like, no matter how angry you might be with God, he will still give you the air you breathe and the sun you crave that shines down upon you.

Blind faith is, knowing that God has your best interest at heart, even though you may be going through some very difficult and challenging times.

You know how much God loves you?

He loves you even though you might be angry or disappointed with Him because He took your loved one to Heaven. He is taking care of not only you, but the ones you love most, those who have left you behind here on earth, while they have moved into that really cool place, we call Heaven.

As much as you love your kids or pets, unconditionally, God loves you just as much! Your kids might do wrong, but you'll be there to help them or defend them regardless of the circumstances. Your kids might be struggling to make ends meet, but you'll do whatever you can to give them what you have, even if you can't afford it.

You will pay for the operation that your adorable pet may need, even if it is unaffordable. Then there is going to be that time where you want to keep your pets here with you, even when they are older and or sickly and you have to make that decision to have them put down because you love them too much to see them suffer any longer.

A new puppy or a newborn child will love you unconditionally, regardless of your choices.

God loves you even more!

For all these people and animals/pets you love so much.

God's love for you is even greater.

Your kids or friends may be angry with you, but in your own weird way, you still love them.

God loves them and you, even more.

Unconditional love is where you'll be able to forgive someone who has done you wrong or anyone else wrong.

There are times where people might not understand you. You feel alone, like people misinterpret your intentions, but God understands and loves you unconditionally. Regardless of your choices, you are always loved and welcomed. Even when you feel alone and you want to give up, or that no one cares, God and your Angels love you so much and with so much compassion, they will never leave your side.

God doesn't beat us up, we beat ourselves up out of guilt, unworthiness, or frustration. Through your negative thoughts come your negative actions; through your negative actions come your negative outcomes. Karma is caused by our actions. Karma is it destiny or fate, cause and effect. Whatever you put out there in the Universe, you will experience right back at you one way or another. You may not see or experience the cause and effect right away but give it time and you will. Timing is everything.

Be forgiving. Let go of your anger. Let go of your resentments, your hate, and your frustrations. If you hold on to all these negative thoughts and vibrations it will not help you get the positive results you're looking for.

If you're looking to make vanilla angel food cake, you'll need vanilla ingredients. You can't make vanilla cake with chocolate ingredients.

Ask God and your Angels for help and allow yourself to receive when help comes to you from any or all directions.

There was an old lady walking in the parking lot, leaving the mall one cold night. It wasn't until she got to her car that she realized that she locked her keys in there. In that moment, out of desperation, she prayed to God in her thoughts for some kind of miracle.

A minute later, a young man was walking by her and noticed that she looked nervous and upset. He asked her if she needed help. The old lady explained that she locked her keys in her car and doesn't know what to do. He said, "Give me a moment, I'll be right back."

This young man ran to his car and grabbed a tool. Within 30 seconds, he got her car door open. She was so grateful, she gave him a big hug and said, "Thank you so much, you are such a kind young man!" The young man sadly replied, "No, I am not, I just got out of jail yesterday."

She moved closer and hugged him harder as she whispered, "Thank you God for sending me a professional!"

BEING RESPONSIBLE vs BEING IRRESPONSIBLE

To make your life easier, just go with what feels right.

Learn to trust and follow your first gut instinct.

People who constantly ask other people for advice, most of the time have no confidence. They give away their power, but then will complain to you if things go wrong and take no responsibility of their choices.

Then there are the crazy people who are always asking for advice and then they do the direct opposite of what is told to them. These types of people are known as an "askhole"

DO SOMETHING ABOUT IT

Stop beating yourself up from those moments of regret, of what you wish you once did. Now is a good time to start doing those things to make things right and make up for lost time.

JESUS, JEWISH, HEAVEN

It makes me laugh inside when people say to me, "If you want to go to Heaven, you need to accept Jesus in your life as your Lord and Savior." But, yet by the same people I was told, and it is understood, that Jesus was/is Jewish.

If Jesus were raised Jewish and lived his life as a Jew, why would that thought process not be good enough for everyone else, for those who do believe in Jesus.

I was also told that the Jewish people are the chosen ones because God delivered the Ten Commandments to Moses and the Jewish people.

The reality is, no one is better than anyone else, we were all created in the image of God. We are all the children, sons, and daughters of God. So, to my understanding, Jesus was and is one of many beautiful souls sent to us, here on Earth, to teach us the highest level of love and integrity.

Moses brought to us the Ten Commandments to abide by the laws of God. Jesus lived his life with pure, unconditional love, taught us, showed us how to be so we can all live our life with the highest integrity and be happy.

If we all live our lives according to the Ten Commandments, if we all live our lives according to the way Jesus lived and thought, then yes, we would all live a happy life and we will all end up going to Heaven. It isn't just about believing in Jesus or living through Jesus but believing in all his loving concepts that He has for God, humanity and life itself.

For all of you who choose to believe in Jesus as your God or your Savior, God Bless you! For all of you who choose to believe in God or life in your own loving ways, regardless of your religious or spiritual way of living or your belief system, God Bless you, too.

Because when it is all said and done... we will all meet up in Heaven one day.

WE ARE ALL ONE

Sad but true. Religion separates us from one another.

People who live for their Religious beliefs tend to believe their way of thinking is better than everyone else's. No matter what Religion you are, people who are truly spiritual believe we are all equal and one with our creator

Reality check: Ask yourself, what do you think is more important in God's eyes,
being Religious or spiritual? Spirituality is the bridge to help Religious people get to God's Kingdom.

Love and spirituality has no limitations or boundaries.

Religion creates boundaries, fears, control, and judgment.

The bottom line is… show love, kindness and respect to your fellow man and yourself and you won't go wrong.

MAKING A LIVING ISN'T NECESSARILY MAKING A LIFE

Whether it be emotionally or financially, too many of us are in that survival mode. It's great when you can work many hours and you're taking care of your family's financial needs as well as your own. Too many people have made their lifestyle going from home to work and work to home without having any quality time for themselves, family, or friends.

While you're busting your ass non-stop doing nothing but taking care of responsibilities for everyone else, there is no reason for you to carry any guilt whatsoever, to take quality time out for yourself at least once a week or every other week. Take that time to do for you whatever brings you joy.

You worked hard for it; you deserve it. Give yourself a bubble bath, go to the gym, go to the movies, out for dinner, listen to live music, see a comedy show, attend a concert, or a ball game, visit people you love to see...why not? Seriously! Why not?

You're willing to pull out all the stops for everyone else and make magic happen for them!! why not do it for yourself?! Why are you holding back?!

This has to do with self-worthiness issues.

Again, you pull out all the stops for everyone else, but when it comes to you, you justify and get practical on yourself, you end up doing very little or nothing at all when it comes to you.

You're probably thinking, "Oh, that's a waste of time I don't need to spend the money, I can use that money to help someone else out or pay some more bills." That's a responsible move, but borrrring! With these kind of moves, with this kind of thought process, you're making a living and not making a life.

Are you really happy by making these kinds of choices?

The word 'practical' and the word 'fun' usually isn't in the same sentence, I'm just saying...

Honor yourself. Love yourself. Respect yourself. This is what will bring you to be a much happier person. I'm not telling you to be irresponsible or completely selfish. All I'm saying is start creating more balance in your life and give yourself self-love.

You deserve it!

YOU WANT TO START YOUR OWN BUSINESS?

Before you start your own business, it is best that you work for someone else, doing what you love to do. Learn the ropes and the tricks from someone who has already been there and done that. There is no better education than learning through experience. Allow yourself to not only do your job well but learn how to properly handle and service the public. Learn how to deal with problems and circumstances when they arise. Learn how to respectfully work along with your co-workers or associates. Learn common courtesies of everyone you're dealing with, how to negotiate, handle the accounting work.

If you want to be successful, you need to go all out and give your best effort and energy forward.

Marketing is a major key to success. Besides doing a great job, properly and professionally marketing yourself is a must. Otherwise, you will never reach your true potential and be as successful as you'd like.

If you want to get ahead, you have to take chances.

If you don't know how to utilize social media, you need to hire someone responsible

who is good and knows how to market and spread the word about you and your products or services.

If you don't yet have the money to market yourself, you should borrow the money or maybe you can barter your services with someone who can help you out.

Don't be afraid to ask people who are very successful on how they became successful. Pick their brain to get valuable information. Offer to buy them lunch or dinner for their time. Keep an open mind. Go to seminars to learn new or better techniques at doing what you do.

If you're having a bad day, stop what you're doing. Relax for the rest of the day or do something fun or positive for yourself to air out your brains and start fresh and new on the next day.

Everyone buys everything based on emotions. When you want to sell your products or services, be enthusiastic. Positive energy is very contagious.

Many years ago, I started a cleaning business. My client, Simon, was giving me some really good business advice that I have never forgotten. He told me, "Artie, always remember, whenever you sell your products or services, you first need to sell yourself. If people like you, they will buy whatever you're selling." So, I went home, and I told my wife what Simon said about me selling myself. I told her, "I made so much money today selling myself that I never got to the product!" Lol!

KEY TO MAKING A RELATIONSHIP WORK

The key ingredient to making a relationship healthy is communication and compromise. Well, yeah, love and trust ranks up there too. LOL!

A lot of people have a habit of not saying things when they're upset. They rather keep quiet and not rock the boat. In the meantime, the resentments are building up inside and you're thinking that your friend, child, or partner should know what you're thinking or how they're hurting you. The reality is, they have no clue unless you say something to them. You need to speak up! Not everyone is a mind reader or psychic.

You assume they should know and most people, who assume things about other people, are wrong.

When you calmly speak your mind to express your thoughts or emotions to whomever you're dealing with, you're at least giving them a chance to understand you. After you say what you need to say and they're still not accommodating to you or agreeing with you, your next words should be, "Ok, what's the compromise?"

If the other person is not willing to compromise with you, you have two choices...

1. You take control of the matters into your own hands and make moves for yourself that best serve your needs, not including them.

Or...

2. You let go of that relationship all together if you are consistently getting let down by that person.

Why torture yourself based on someone else's actions if they don't take your feelings or position into consideration.

There are many times where two or more people may agree that they disagree on certain matters and that's fine, that's ok. As long as there is a mutual level of respect for one another and everyone knows where everyone stands.

Do you compromise, or do you let go? That choice is yours.

THE IMPORTANCE OF POSITIVE INTENTIONS

When you pray for other people's good health and well-being, you automatically get blessed in return. Wish good things upon others and good things will happen to you. Wishing ill or negativity upon others, negativity will come right back at you and bite you in the ass.

If you have one thousand drops of water in the same glass, each drop of water is now mixed as one. Each drop as a whole holds the same energy, same value, and the same quality as all the other drops of water in that same glass. If you taint a few drops of water and mix it in with the rest of the water, all the other drops will be tainted as well. Energy is contagious, whether it be good or bad. That's why it is important to keep the positive energy flowing in your life. When giving positive loving energy to others as well as yourself, you're simultaneously blocking out negative energy. So, now good energy can work its magic and make good positive outcomes happen for you in your favor as well as for others that you wish or pray for.

Our souls are all created from the same energy source, that energy source is known as God or the Universe, whichever way feels more comfortable for you to say.

It is what it is. Amen!

LOVE IS BLIND

Without question, when your emotions are high, all intelligence, smarts, and logic go right out the window.

When people are in love, they tend to look at the ones they love through 'Rose colored glasses. They can do no wrong according to one's perception because you want what you want so bad with the other person, you will make up any excuse to make the one you love not look so bad. Even if that person is still taking advantage of you, hurting you in some way, or lying to you, your blind love will still make excuses to cover up for them.

People who are not as emotionally involved or invested, can usually see the truth more clearly. It's not until the trust is broken or the pain becomes too great and the person being hurt decides that they're not going to take it anymore. The person who is doing the abusing will usually belittle their partner and make them feel like they are stupid, the bad person, or crazy. They manipulate their partner to feel as if they don't know what they're talking about, can't do anything right, and everything is always all their fault when things go wrong. However, the abuser in the relationship will take no responsibility for anything that is wrong. They will create excuses for everything, making any given situation not their fault, but blame their partner. The abuser will often say things to their partner, "Who's gonna want you?" or "I'm the best you can get!" or "You are worthless without me!"

When you step back for a little while, away from that relationship that you're not happy with, you'll finally be able to see the truth about the person who caused you all that hurt and pain. Hopefully at that point you'll have the courage to respect yourself and no longer be a victim. Walk away from that abusive relationship! You need to get out of that unhealthy environment and be with people who support you and/or love you. Stepping out of an unhealthy relationship will help you see the truth and reality of your life and life itself.

Another aspect of love is unconditional love. When you love and care for someone so much, you can see there's something good in that person that no one else can appreciate, it is your dying love and support that doesn't give up on the one you love. You want to help them get rid of their demons and get through their challenges in life. However, if the person who is down and out doesn't want to help themselves, all the love and help in the world won't save them. They have to want to heal and accept the help for themselves.

Unconditional love is also when you love someone for who they are and not just what they can do for you. Unconditional love is the passion you have for someone and no matter what, if they need you, you will be there for them. Unconditional love is regardless of one's mistakes; you're not judging them and still love them with all your heart.

You should not feel guilty about the ones you couldn't save; it was out of your control. Their problems are between them and God.

TO BE LOVED

Unfortunately, a lot of us first learn about love through the painful experiences of what love is not. When that unusual feeling of true love genuinely does step into your life, you should embrace it and don't make the mistake of pushing it away. It's what you always wanted, understandably your inner child was afraid of rejection. Your confidence and worthiness issues made you feel like you weren't worth being loved at all and that's not true! The reality is you are very much worthy of being loved!

You may have had times where you experienced that people or a specific person that you wanted love from the most, were just incapable of giving or expressing love to you in the way that you wanted or deserved. The reason why you didn't receive that kind of love from them isn't because you weren't good enough or you didn't deserve it, but because they themselves, the abusers, never experienced being loved in that way while growing up. So how can they share their love with you or anyone else in that way if they rarely or never experienced love for themselves? They just don't have it within them to give.

Just because you're not used to being loved, doesn't mean you should push it away when it is expressed to you by others. No matter how old you are, please allow that inner child within you to be loved and nurtured in a way you have always imagined and wished for.

When you allow your heart to open up to be loved, you will finally know and experience that feeling of what it is like to be loved and how it was always meant to be. When you allow the feeling of love into your heart, you can then give the best loving vibrations of who you are, to others. Do yourself a favor, embrace love when it is there right in front of you. Now do everyone else a favor, share your love with them.

Amen!!

103

THE END, MY FRIEND

Made in the USA
Middletown, DE
14 January 2022

58291180R00066